BASIC BIGFOOT RESEARCH & GUIDE TO

KNOWING THE TRUTH

AUTHOR
DANIEL J. BENOIT

Est. 2014

Basic Bigfoot Research

& Guide to Knowing The Truth

Author & Wildlife Researcher

Daniel J. Benoit

ABOUT THE BOOK

First of all this book is for everyone believer or non .

Researching and Making True Discoveries of Natures hidden Legend The Sasquatch , known as the Elusive Bigfoot that many do not acknowledge do to the lack of Research and having the closed mind as most do.

This book is to bring awareness and enlighten their minds on the truth and why they should believe in what really is out there. This book speaks on the history of some of the reports and sightings through out the past history and the documented knowledge made by our Native Americans dating over a hundred plus years .

I will also show you in this book the scientific studies of research that I myself have done to show you of the many known primates and their behaviors to give you the illustrations of what's happening in our own neck of the woods and what is really creating what is found by the naked eye but so many over look the reality of life and nature. Its time to open your mind and eyes people and stop ignoring the Facts.

To clarify I don't claim to know everything and I am far from perfect but I dedicate my time into learning and gathering information. I value your thoughts & concerns. I hope to provide more clearer Evidence as I continue on my Research .

ENJOY

IS EVERYONE A LIER

This is a serious question and we must take into great consideration that not everyone is a liar . Consider this as well the long history of reports and the ones who have come forward to share what they have

seen and have encountered.

Some reports and stories can be easily dismissed or ruled out as misidentifications However with the overall look into all reports with some coming from Police officers and many outdoors men who know how to properly Identify a subject of nature and also with a trained eye as well ; this is a very great observation of detail of visual evidence and proof but many who do not believe will mock them to a point of saying they are seeking attention or making up camp stories sort of say, But wake up people these reports date back over a hundred years plus in the past up to recent days as of now.

Records of all known animals and wildlife are kept and also acknowledged by our own Native Americans of every tribe through out North America and into Canada , & Alaska as well. We understand that the Natives are very Spiritual but at the same time they are very serious and Speak wisdom , We have learned a lot from them over a course of time but what or how do they look at Sasquatch ? Well he is as a guardian of the forest or a Big brother Indian who means to brings peace to the land .

Think about this as well ; If you have a friend or even a close relative whom you highly respect and trust and they come to you with a claim of seeing a Sasquatch and knew it was nothing else known to mankind ; Would you laugh or mock them because you "Think" there is No such thing?

We know that bears exist but how many of you have seen them? Not many of you but some who have not seen them believe so but still have not seen with there own eyes. The same concept goes along with the living Sasquatch or Bigfoot with many today. Some of us have seen only by accident or coincidence but according to Native Americans it is a blessing to see one meaning it is meant to be meaning for to have one reveal itself it may bring you peace and knowledge .

For those who claim to see them at night but with no visual of the whole figure of their body but only clear eye shine this is a much harder concept of understanding or believing from others. Just to mention a few qualities and or traits to observe or know of is simply the height of the eyes the space between the eyes the movement they portray as far as head movement . And is the counter observer showing curious actions or simple Primate behaviors ? Remember its important to rule out the known species of the specific area your researching or having your encounters. This will really shed a lot of light on the truth behind the mystery and as you continue to read onward you will see how I will speak of ruling out the obvious. And for all you attention seekers and Bigfoot enthusiasts if you want bragging rights Be honest with yourself and with others . We do not have time to waste on hoaxing.

WHAT IS SASQUATCH & IS THERE PROOF ?

Well many theories flood the world with these Questions and to share a few before I speak the truth of What they really are , Do keep in mind that the a following are only theories and assumptions not facts.

Some believe in the Extraterrestrial theory meaning not of this world, Sorry but its clear and safe to say that those who believe in such are out of this world themselves. Some believe that they are part of early man (Homo Sapien) - aka - (Cave men) during the Prehistoric era, Well science teaches this Theory of the existence of such form of men well this part of referring to the existence I do agree or believe but to say that Sasquatch is of this origin – No I do Not agree, However if science was to acknowledge the existence of Bigfoot and was to classify such creatures in this order – This would clearly contradict their Evolutionary theory Saying Man went from man to Ape , Instead ape to man. Well to clarify my standings on all this I do not agree nor believe in any part of the Evolution theory. Now into reality if you want to put it this way – Lets look at the prehistoric era and what is it that did exist so many years ago: Primates of so many different species were here since the Beginning of time along with all the other animals but One specific primate literally stood out but yet taller than most others He is also not acknowledged or known to many people because they do not pay attention to the Prehistoric history or era. Well my friends allow me to Introduce to you (Gigantopithecus) a 9 to 10 foot tall standing walking upright Primate who roamed the earth back during this time , but it is more logical to believe that this species is what still exists today . We do know that many of our known animals living today date back from the prehistoric era so why rule this out ? I believe that today's Bigfoot(s) are the descendants of this large massive primate but some may be of a different breed giving the various sizes reported through out the regions or states of our Country. Breeds ? Yes you read this correct – Almost every species known to mankind has a different breed within its kind , horses, dogs, cats, fish, and Especially Primates. So if your asking me what is a Bigfoot : I am telling you my belief and the reason behind my belief is the history of origin , history of reported observations with details shared repeatedly over the years with consistent descriptions etc.

Sasquatch is a Primate and believed to be a descendant of Gigantopithecus but perhaps of a possible different Breed.

I stand my ground on this and it will be proven in time, regardless if its done by me or anyone else.

Do you feel different ? If so Why – What research did You do – What results have you Discovered ?

Lets classify the species shall we ; Sure why not Science may not agree or so wouldn't the many other extremest of the community but their the ones that are stuck up with the blind side of science and also the ignorance of simple understanding . So here we go if it acts , behaves , looks, lives as a primate then what is the problem with calling it a primate ? I will tell you why science will not classify it this way because they themselves are no more than lab rats stuck in the lab and with all their high tech educational brain waves and are far set apart from reality and nature. Very few of them step foot out in the field and spend dedicated time observing and learning the hands on and visual appearance of the life as it is displayed for us . I clearly know of one Anthropologist who is dedicated in learning the truth of these creatures as much as many of us do, But this Gentleman clearly states with out reason of doubt that there is simply a large unclassified primate living among us . In his studies and observations as well as his analyzing of the many foot casts brought to his attention for research he has found and discovered that these casts display the Dermal ridges of a Non human Primate.

This Gentleman is better known as <u>Dr. Jeff Meldrum</u> of the Idaho State University & Allow me also to introduce you to a Former forensic finger examiner (Law officer) <u>Jimmy Chillcutt</u> who as well studied along side together with Meldrum to examine the Sasquatch foot casts and who has found the Dermal ridge patterns as well to be consistent with many of the casts belonging to a Non Human primate. He is convinced and states with confidence that there is a Living primate among us as well. To learn more of Mr. Chillcutt and his work related to Jeff Meldrum I highly recommend the Purchase of a great book pointing out all the evidence studied and laid out for us by Author Jeff Meldrum –

SASQUATCH: LEGEND MEETS SCIENCE

PROOF

And to speak on proof – Well lets keep it short sweet and simple here Ladies & Gentlemen with what we just spoke on above and what I shared pretty much sums it up to a degree . We have Foot casts with Dermal Ridge patterns belonging to a Primate , The FBI has examined and tested Hair samples but with no Match found in any database , Multiple eye witness accounts with descriptions being consistent abroad, and If we shall Lets even bring up the Film footage of Roger Patterson & Bob Gimlin – So many have attacked that footage and can not prove it to be faked , But keep in mind that the foot casts found on site were found to be authentic as well. Remember Our Native Americans and their long history of Acknowledgment of the existence of Sasquatch , But Science is too ignorant to acknowledge it – A body is the most Logical sense of proof according to so many & that may be so – I do not disagree with that however know that Bigfoot is an Endangered species and very rare at that So I feel that this must be taken in a different direction when it comes to providing a body, We need to continue in our research and find other ways of providing such evidence.

Photo's , Video's , Hair DNA , Foot prints etc. are all the various signs of proof we do have but even the DNA does not seem enough for scientific research. Perhaps with enough Field research we just may come across the remains of one but we must stay at it and I will tell you this that the E.C.B.R.O. Is in the process of doing all of this with the DISCOVERY PROJECT , in effect and the whole team is out constantly Investigating and researching to bring you what we need to shed light on this subject.

A question most asked: Where is the body or remains:

FOOD FOR THOUGHT- Nature creates a natural blanket as I call it with the seasons to hide a lot on the ground as well from the seasons pasts (LEAF LITTER) before I get into this discussion I want to bring up the Existence of Bears again – We know they are real although not everyone has seen them especially in their own environment But Let me ask you this before going on any further , **" How many of you have found Bears that Died of Natural cause ?"** Well I do believe I can answer this for you (NONE) I can quote from **Loren Coleman's** Book **BIGFOOT: THE TRUE STORY OF APES IN AMERICA:** By part of a reply from **Grover Krantz**; In Regards to the 1st Question found on page 236 : *If Bigfoot is real, Why hasn't anyone found a dead Bigfoot Yet?* Now the best population estimate guess we can make is there are at least one hundred bears for every one Bigfoot: with that being said or stated I would like to believe or say this just may be Slightly accurate however of whatever the numbers are in comparison to the many Sightings and reports with today's database we may have more Bigfoot than we think , This has not been proven in any form of study but back into my study when it comes to bears and Bigfoot I do compare them a lot together for a few good reason's and One ; their Elusiveness, Two their eating habits , Three their Living / Sleeping habits And Four their dark fur or hair . The two species are completely different when it comes to what they are but are also often both misidentified in the field by the untrained eye. Many report seeing a Sasquatch when only seeing a bear – **Why is this ?** The two are known to be biped but know this that a Bigfoot is Always known to be Biped although some reports claim to see them on all Fours and that Can easily mean a Misidentified Bear, But a bear is only Biped for a short while and has been known to do this to reach food or Intimidation to scare off predators. Bears can not run while Biped and can only take a few short steps at the most, & Know that they are (**QUADRO PEDS**) meaning a four limb walking animal, So Caution when making your claims know what you are observing . Study the appearance of the subject Height , Length of Limbs and Look at the Ears are they on top or on the side of the head ? **Why the Ears ?** Bears have ears that stand out on the top of their heads and Bigfoot have ears like any other Primate (Human or Non Human) Common sense but basic understanding remember that bears have Paws and have toes on both front and rear But their Feet are almost as the length of Humans but more oval and wider and again they do have Toes that are rounded .

(MORE INFO IN THE RESEARCH & STUDY SECTION IN THIS BOOK)
SEE THE ILLUSTRATIONS FOR BASIC COMPARISON IN THE
REFERANCE SECTION :

SIGNS , STRUCTURES & FORMATIONS

For those who are actually observant of their surroundings when out in the field you may be noticing a lot of art work and shelter like patterns and designs as well as very odd findings in nature. Are you finding trees ripped open or clawed at ? Are you finding Tee Pee like structures big and small , Are you finding bent or twisted trees and snapped limbs ? Are you or have you ever found two trees Laid together to form a large X in the most oddest place ? Well in this section you will learn what it is that may be doing this . We have a few suspects and they are all responsible for each of their own . See photo illustrations of a few examples found in the Bedding & formation section and what I have alone is nothing compared to what else is out there.

OK to start this off I am going to bring up the subject of **Weather** and how this plays a great role in the formation of many structures found in Nature , Notice how trees that are up rooted have roots not far into the ground ; Between the wet ground from the rain which causes a weak setting or base and softness of the ground and the Wind that causes a lot of movement among the Trees and all the other plants Etc. So Heavy wind and hard rain are the key factors in most up Rooted trees and Yes the wind forms or creates bent and snapped trees and Limbs as well , But lets look at other Suspects or Causes of these happenings , I again must bring up the **Bear .** These creatures Love to play with tree saplings , Climb trees , and while playing with the trees they are known to bend them over and snap the weak trees and Limbs . Keep in mind bears are very strong and some are much heavier than others and their weight can also be the cause of bent and snapped trees and limbs.

Note that bears will also use limbs and other fallen timber for bedding – the appearance of these bedding styles are as if you had a brush pile just started. And another fact about bears when it comes to seeing Old, Dead or Rotted trees or Logs laying down with chunks removed or shredded apart are the signs of a hungry bear seeking out bugs , grubs , worms , etc that all dwell in these rotted logs, and Don't be fooled by over turned stones – It is not Bigfoot doing that – again it is only bears doing the same thing with the logs except with the stones , Looking for insects . (FOOD)

Now I want to get back into the Bent & Snapped trees and limbs we discussed how weather is the key factor in this but there is a much greater cause among us but with a more distinct appearance of damage. There are patterns and formations created by Sasquatch forming Shelters , Nests, and other signs commonly done among the known primates in the world, and you will learn why and for what reasons they do such things. First I want to get you to identify and become familiar with the differences between Weather damage and Sasquatch damage.

Lets look at trees approximately 4" to 5" round or some even a little larger they may be bent but look for a serious twist at the breaking point or angle , The tree will be twisted in either direction

(Research Credit – **Fred Kanney**) but whats more distinct is if its twisted like a cork screw

(Research Credit - **Larry Davis**) . Sometimes from the twist you will see a split or separation at the break area. I personally have found a tremendous amount of these in various areas through out my Field Research , But think about it for second – How is this done especially if the trees are strong and large , Well your average chimpanzee has the strength of 10 men and their bodies are made of 90% muscle compared to body fat, so picture a 7 – 8' tall Sasquatch weighing up to 700 lbs and just imagine the strength one may have to cause such damage. I do believe if your reading this illustration correctly the Facts speak for themselves. ***Why Do Sasquatch Do this damage ?*** Well if we understand and know about why our

Known primates do this its simple; One reason is Intimidation, to scare off an intruder , And or the start of a structure. Various markings such as X's are signs of a Dominant male or female that inhabits that territory and its a fair warning for others to stay away. Now this is the way to look at it in a Primate state of sense , although we have so much yet to learn of these Creatures these signs and formations May have an entirely other sense of meaning , A few individuals try to say that Bent or twisted trees or Limbs are forms of directional's when we have no foundation to go by or base this theory on so how can this be of any truth, Just from one rumor or ones say so This has become some what of a wide spread assumption that has not been proven. Another Structure I want to discuss briefly is the Tee Pee or **(Tri-pod)** as I call it . This is very interesting and for some reason is an awesome find to come across for me , But This has been found in various styles but all are built similar to one another. You will see these usually with Three trees at a Minimum joined together at the top while the bottoms are spread apart and outward . Sometimes these formations will include other trees joined with them , and another thing is Look at the bottoms of each trees that form the structure and look at the root ball and see if it has been pushed over from its planted spot or has it been put there from another location. To debunk if this from a natural weather cause Examine the trees around the area and above the structure to see if it has fallen or snapped off another tree. Pay close attention to that too, There is no telling how old the formations may be as far as length of time it was built , You can not go by the age or deadness of the tree it self either. **WHY ?** Because who or whatever created the formations may have used dead fallen timbers to begin with , so in this case there is no telling how long it has been there **UNLESS** you are in a general area that you normally hike or research and know the layout or landscape of the land itself and notice or observe the changes from the time frame you go through that area then you can determine how old it is. That is basic common sense and there will be more brought up in regards to Observations in the Research section or page of this book. One more thing I want to bring up is Stacked rocks ; this is something found by many individuals who believe that Bigfoot does this, well It has not been proven but this is also done by hikers , campers, & hunters to mark trails, So till we learn more on this stay tuned. The possibilities can not be ruled out just yet !

RESEARCH & STUDY

In this section I plan to make a recap of most of what I went over but a little more in depth However I will most likely get into topics I have not covered as well. In this section I will boldly state facts that some may question but this book speaks for it self and so does the research .

Lets again start off with our history of Sasquatch here alone in North America , the first acknowledgments of Sasquatch begin with Our Native Americans , who Once Lived in peace in harmony before the Invasion of outsiders who began to populate the land . The Natives were very knowledgeable knew of every known animal who inhabited the forests around them , Every known animal known to The Natives were documented by drawings . And even the History and stories of old were past down through Generations and still are. And over the years leading up to modern times reports have began to slowly pop up as populations grew and Logging companies started to open up the forests and the more outdoors men explored reports and signs of Evidence started to come about. For those unaware President Teddy Roosevelt has even reported actually seeing a Sasquatch during one of his Hunting excursions. He knew it was not a bear.

Then In 1967 the first yet greatest visual Evidence of Sasquatch was caught on Film and many of us know this footage as the Roger Patterson & Bob Gimlin Film and the subject on film was defined as a Female Bigfoot with the details of Breasts upon the front chest .

KNOW *THE FACTS*

Sasquatch or Bigfoot although Science has not classified the obvious these creatures are Primates in the Flesh and are very strong animals. These Primates are the descendants of the Gigantopithecus ; Again Who was this Animal ? He was a 9 to 10 foot tall walking upright Primate during the Prehistoric time period . The Bigfoot species are just as any other Primate (Human or Non) we are all flesh and Blood Creatures that posses NO special abilities that some outrageously claim . Primates display a great deal of intelligence some more than others.

When we look at what evidence is available – Ask yourself " Is this Enough " Well what exactly do we have available ? Foot Prints of Human like tracks but Not human; cast and analyzed & the Casts displaying primate dermal ridge patterns , Visual evidence on Film , DNA samples of hair, & scat coming back as Not known after being tested – Even from the FBI , Unnatural Tree or stick formations & Damage - (Primate related) , Vocalizations - (Primate related) Well I would say honestly Yes it should be but unfortunately for Science It is NOT.

And while we are on the subject of Evidence in this Research Section – I again will bring up the Question of " Where is the body or remains ? A commonly asked questions among skeptics or the mocking non believer. There is some basic knowledge that I must bring to your attention regarding the ecology and the effects that Acidic soil has on the perseverance of bones and the break down process with a dead or decaying corpse . I will take you step by step as simple and as clear as possible on this subject.

TAPHONOMY – Is the process that takes place when death becomes of any living subject or being and we will discuss how the breakdown of decay runs its course.

There is three stages of the breakdown process first is the **LIVOR MORTIS** stage where the blood in the body flows into one settling place or pool within the body , Second we have the **RIVOR MORTIS** stage , All the muscular tissue becomes rigid & incapable of relaxing , And thirdly we come to the **ALGOR MORTIS** stage , The body loses heat and cools down. Following these stages the body goes into **BLOAT** or swelling of the body where gases are formed by *(Microbes)* growing rapidly and as the body breaks down and decays away we then enter into the **SKELETONIZATION**

process , the decay of bones is very important especially with Archeologist . The soil plays an extremely big roll in this process. Now depending on area or location of the country that obtains or gets a lot of rain fall the soil may hold a great deal of **ACID** in which creates ACIDIC SOIL . Well a lot of area's remain damp or you may have area's that have a great abundant vegetation growth this is from the high level of Acid in the soil that produces healthy looking and full grown and bright green trees and various plant life . Well when it comes to the Acidic Soil this is not healthy to the bones of course – **WHY ?** Well think about it – What does Acid do to clothes for example – Well with bones it produces a faster decomposition process ; It eats up the bones breaking them down to become the soil itself. Its like that saying Ashes to ashes dust to dust sort of say. And to add to this whole process weather plays a part in this , with the temperature as well , the heat will speed all this up to break down faster.

So I really hope this may bring some understanding and basic knowledge to your mind and give you something to think about. Oh and I am not done explaining about body remains just yet ; I told you earlier in this book that I will be bringing up bears again and how I compare them to Bigfoot well there is another comparison I have to share with you on that matter. Well we discussed on how bear remains are not recovered well with bears They know there time of death or when it approaches , so they have there place(s) of where they Lie down and depart from this world and I believe they are hidden with help from others, but keep in mind with any other dead animals remains are scavenged off by other critters of the forest, Well with Bigfoot when one becomes of death they are part of clans or not far from the others and their remains are hidden and not to be found . This is known in the Primate world , Another Primate like a Chimpanzee for example will carry or drag the dead one around till they dispose of it For the very fact they are close to their lost ones and have feelings as we Humans do. Alot of this is clearly overlooked by many who fail to understand the known primates. Now I will mention a theory , of course it is only a theory , and not proven but We know that the known primates have been known to be cannibalistic to others , We do not know if Bigfoot is the same way although in some Native Traditions they claim of there Sasquatch legends being this way, Such as the **MICMAC** Indian tribe from out of Canada and into Maine.

WHERE DID THE NAME (SASQUATCH) COME FROM

Well most of us know its an Indian Name , So lets be more specific on the origin of it . The language is of the Halkomelom spoken or used by the Coastal Salish Indian tribe The name itself originates from the word *Sesquac* . ***Canadian Journalist J.W. Burns*** coined the name or term Sasquatch to Refer to all Giving names of the various Native tribes regardless of what name they each have for the Bigfoot. This is not changing the Name but only used when referring to a Bigfoot in General. I can go into naming a few related to the various tribes but to name them all would be another whole topic. There is approximately around 60 plus names and that is not including the nick names giving by so many , such as the wood booger , the Skunk ape, Big hairy man, And the wild man or women of the woods just to name a few for examples.

WHAT SHOULD YOU KNOW WHEN RESEARCHING

Well any one who is either just getting started or has been doing this for a good period of time , I will share some basic knowledge on what you should know if you don't already; First of all I recommend you choosing an area to become both familiar & Comfortable with , get to know this area real well. You want to be very observant of your area at all times and be cautious as well. A good researcher notices change each time he/she returns to the area , Examine the change , document your findings , Use a Camera or if available use A video camcorder , Film and record your area for future research purposes to compare possible future changes as well. When scouting the area constantly stop , look , & listen , Scan your eyes all around you and listen as you do this. One important reason why you need to do is not just to try to find Evidence in the field but become aware of any possible danger in the area of predators , such as bears, mountain lions, cougars , bob cats , and Even Venomous snakes that may dwell around the area , All these are known to blend in well with nature especially the subject that we are Researching. And as far as Listening , Listen for movement , & Vocalizations .

The best time for Sasquatch to be active is at night when most of the forest becomes alive , I have heard a majority of my Vocalizations late at night between the hours of 10pm and 1am . Sasquatch in various area's will communicate to others by howls, wails, and whoops. , A lot of Coyote howls are mistaken for Bigfoot so listen carefully.

Finding & Collecting potential Evidence is always awesome if you can rule out the other known animals and know how to Identify the various species and their Scat , foot tracks etc. Yes Identifying and knowing the differences between all other animals that inhabit the area is very crucial in conducting field research . First you want to know what inhabits the area , and become familiar with their habits, such as when they come and go , what they eat, where they may be bedding , This is what Field researchers do . Anyone who claims to be a Real Bigfoot researcher here is a question for you; Are you doing all the above ? How can you research something that is not known or completely understood when you have no clue of the known and obvious. You can most likely just be fooling yourself as well as others with your outrageous claims. Researchers are Biologists who study various topics and learn about the ecology and have understanding about Nature as a whole, We study and learn about the various wildlife as well and their behaviors , patterns , & habits . Its not hard to start learning or to get familiar with all this . But with all the above said I will say this – To conduct serious research there is three things to know and remember that you must do & need : Observations in the field, Dedication in this Line or work, and Perseverance.

LANGUAGE & COMMUNICATIOS OF PRIMATES

Well this is interesting , but if we were to strictly go by hear say then yes but to me its just a theory or rumor, although a few through their research and audio recordings have claimed to have captured short broken up phrases , Researcher **Fred Kanney** speaks up on this Quoting that he has Recordings stating that he has picked up responses replying to his Questions while out in the field
" *Are you here* " & " *Where are you* " and the replies were as follows *(Yup & We are here)* So unless this was a Misidentified sound we can not rule it out entirely , Fred Kanney is also one among others who claim that the Sasquatch use the Cherokee language dialect , See Fred Kanney for further details on this Subject directly . Now lets again speak of the known primates and their ways of communicating to one another , Wailing out , Screeching , Teeth Chatter, ground slapping, chest pounding, and even reaching out ones hand asking for permission

or rendering submission to another, but keep in mind these are all gestures and forms of communications And Not a Language. Through my research and studies with the known primates of the various sorts No where have I ever come across the mention of them speaking of any kind, But I will say this: It has not been proven that they can not do so & Sasquatch do communicate a lot in the same manner with very similar Gestures and Vocalizations. *Why do Primates howl or wail out ?* And the information I Share goes for Sasquatch as well. Most of the time with this form of communication they are simply locating others of their group or clan as some call it. Known primates also do wood knocking using sticks to hit against the ground or mainly a tree, This is a warning and or form of Intimidation.

RECOGNITIONS

Dr. Jeff Meldrum , John Bindernagel , & Ian Redmond , are the People responsible and who have Influenced me in my Research & Studies .

These Individuals are Great in what they do and Helped me as I follow and learned from them on how to better conduct my Research . They encouraged me to look deeper into specific studies when I am at home in my study outside of the field . I encourage you as well to look into these gentlemen and observe their work , see what they know , and To study into their field a little , I promise you will gain so much more understanding and wisdom .

As founder of the **E.C.B.R.O. - East Coast Bigfoot Researchers Organization** I have come a long ways with my research and have learned a lot by one of the greatest teachers among us all *"EXPERIENCE"* it is there for you as well , Time and dedication is needed to gain this. Through out my journey In all the research in and out of the field I have come to examine many of you that I have met through the web and some in person and I gained a lot through many shared blogs and postings of evidence but I used that in my research to compare to my scientific studies and with field observations I have corrected so much of it in so many ways but it has also opened my eyes to new possibilities as well, there is so much to learn. I have managed to gain great friendships and special bonds of trust among some of you as my fellow researchers that are proudly a part of the ECBRO TEAM . My Team members have displayed great Research ethics and Intelligence in and out of the field. Some are new in the research process and Like them I myself have much more to gain and learn. I have dedicated members who are always out researching and Investigating and Making great discoveries, I want to Thank them for I have gained so much from all of them and I like to believe the feelings mutual , But Special Recognition Goes out to the following: **(Tracy Arnold , Fred Kanney , Samuel Bell Jr. , Cliff Stanley , Larry Davis , Richard Siever , Bill Benoit , Kimi Corbett , & Daren Disorda) & to mention one who is a great Inspiration and encouragement I want to Thank (Muareena Myers) for seeing and understanding my work and cause in & through all this !**

I also want to Include & Thank Mr. Walter Tippie for his support and Sponsor of the ECBRO with His hand crafted leather Bigfoot necklaces (www.etsy.com) also J.M. Bailey and her signed autographed of EVE from the Iron ridge mountain series (www.ironridgemountain.com) Thank you truly all !

And there is so many more to mention that have been also great supporters of the ECBRO and Our Discovery Project (Research Program) and As we continue to bring awareness and educate others of what is necessary to know and understand we hope that you continue to share our research and share your thoughts and concerns with us all .

Feel Free to Visit our Website forums www.ecbro.com and

www.ecbro.wordpress.com

ABOUT THE AUTHOR:

Born on March 25th of 1980 in Milford , Mass. from Douglas , Mass. Moved to Virginia at the age of 12 and grew up down here from an early youth to my current year now. I was always an outdoors boy going out hiking or hunting with dad at a young age and grew up hunting and fishing most of my life. I played sports growing up through my teen age years and became involved with the Martial arts ever since I was real young and after moving to Va I later picked it back up and studied in the Korean style of Martial Arts (Tae Kwon Do) and I did this for 7 years and participated in a few international Martial Arts tournaments achieving 2 first place trophies and a 3rd place trophy and after earning my 1st degree Black belt I went on to become an Instructor of my own class. I became a father in June of 2001 and gained custody of my child since she was 3 months old and Life has brought many lessons as it went by including one in particular that has always been a mysterious thought but an interest in the back of my mind, After seeing a few documentaries on the Study Of Bigfoot and Learning and seeing the Patterson film it had me paying more attention to the outdoors a lot more closely , this is what sparked the overwhelming Passion in me to continue to look into the Mysterious Creature that lives among us. I quietly kept this Great Interest to myself for the longest time and slowly started to Do more in depth studies and more field observations , As I gathered my own evidence and started to see the various patterns I then began to start talking to get inputs and information. I was solo for a while and needed a way to gain more information and find others involved , So that's where facebook came in handy. After creating an account I slowly started to find people and started joining groups to gather up more information and a lot of what I was finding was found by others as well , Then went on to start the Facebook Group the ECBRO which is now a secret group do to the settings However I have other ECBRO groups for others to partake in . Now as far as my educational needs came about I continued in the studies that I started with of (Ecology , Biology , and wildlife research) I later went on to meet seasoned Field Researcher (Fred Kanney) who is actually local to me , who also shared his knowledge with me and we began to research his area and one of my areas of interest as well. We even conducted our own Camping Investigations to seek out Evidence and from there I started a yearly event that will take place Every year in various Locations , States etc. known as the Annual ECBRO camping Expeditions consisting of the ECBRO Team members and anyone else that wants to learn or Share the Experience. I am found on Facebook as Daniel Benoit (ecbro ceo) , on Google+ , and Twitter .

Contact information to Submit a report currently send report to ecbro98@gmail.com and or See anyone of the Team members, The ECBRO is currently seeking individuals who are honest and trust worthy to Represent and to start up in their area. Stay up to date on all the Latest Video blogs and shows on My YouTube channel ECBRO98 . Help support & bring awareness to our Cause.

KNOWING PRIMATES

(NON – HUMAN)
INTRODUCTION

Welcome to the primate learning center of this Research book, In this section you will get a lot more familiar with the various known common primates and will also learn the differences between an **APE & MONKEY** . (see list below)

APES	MONKEYS
1. Gorilla's	1. lemurs
2. Chimpanzee's	2. Baboons
3. Orangutang's	3. Macaque
4. Bonobos	4. Colobus

Ok above is a few of each named but we will go into some details and really get to know all about Apes & Monkey's and Just Primates in general . Although each have their own physical appearance and some have different habits they all have Habits and behaviors in common as well, regardless of what kind of Primate they are.

First Can you tell me What is one thing that Monkeys have that Ape's DO NOT ? Give up …....... Ok no biggy Its a (TAIL) This is one simple way to identify or know the difference between the Two. I will keep this section clear and simple as possible; It is very important that you Learn and Understand about (Non Human) Primates and I will take you step by step by category to get you educated on Our Known Primates . After learning about them then you need to compare the findings and Observations you have done or have yet to do in the Research field. Knowing our known primates will help you understand and know Bigfoot as well. This is often ignored , overlooked , and or simply not known to the average individual who Researches in the Bigfoot Field.

Primates such as the Apes , Monkeys are considered to be our nearest relatives in the world on which I must Agree , However Not according to the Evolutionary theory, I Agree according to the habits , behaviors and Intelligence of these animals , And I will explain all this as you read on in this section. And Know that Primates are also endangered and I will mention why as well.

EVOLUTION
(ONLY A THEORY)

I will explain briefly about what exactly Evolution is. Scientist believe but can not prove that us Humans developed from Monkey's , & Apes So many years ago, One Reason behind this theory is the similar appearance in facial features and hands. I do not believe in this theory . If Evolution is what happened , Then why did it ever stop ? Good Question Right ? Well yes it is and Monkey's and Apes and all other Primates are still what they are today, So how can this even be any bit true. Primates and all other animal Species were of their own kind and still are to this day. Only few species on earth are known to evolve such as Frogs , and Some Lizards to go from aquatic having gills to land and then back to aquatic. I can go on to speak about my true belief on Creation against the Evolution theory but not many believe in that, So to stay on subject I will close on this subject now . My point was made and I stand on my belief.

There is so much to touch up on here to get you to know and understand what you need to know about Primates , So Lets start it off shall we …......

There is great deal of known primates but in the Primate order it is broken up into six natural order groups; The lemurs , the lorises and galagos , the tarsiers , the new world monkey's the old world monkeys , and finally apes and Humans, but to stay more on point I will go on to discuss and explain basic features of the Known primates to give a basic understanding to you as I will go into Known primates and further comparisons to what was mentioned earlier in this book about Bigfoot and the various evidence found among us in the field. My main focus will be on Apes especially and why I choose apes is crucial as well as Substantiating to Show you why Bigfoot is an Ape and nothing more .

Understand that my Scientific Research that you read here is my Evidence shared to you . My field work revealed to me that all my studies all matched up and pieces of the puzzle came together but there is a lot more to the puzzle & is waiting to be unraveled and solved, all I am doing is bringing and presenting to you my basic research and conclusions of all findings that I have made.

Perhaps you need to include your findings and compare them with mine and others and just maybe the missing pieces will fall into place.

So here we go Lets get familiar with the Apes of the world and learn the basics shall we.

BREEDING AMONG APES

Like any other animal this is a natural occurrence that takes place at any time of an Apes life , There is no season or time that this happens ; Just like Humans Mating or Sexual behaviors is all the time or when the male becomes turned on or enticed from the female. The female does have her Menstrual cycle although it is stated that the females may only ovulate once or twice a year depending on species. The males may have up to several partners at a time and therefore producing many offspring . This creates large groups or clans .

During the Breeding stage or when a male seeks out a mate a lot can occur between other males and females. Violent outbursts , such as the male in some primates may become violent or very offensive to fend off other males to keep the group of females to himself making him the dominant one to be able to mate with the females he has chosen. In some cases the female chooses what male will be suitable for her , for example does his group have the more abundance of food and are they healthy, The males in the ape family like larger families unlike the females its not like that. They care about the well being of their groups. There are several signs that will indicate that the female is trying to entice the male such as showing off her swollen rear end or by a simple stair just like in humans. Sometimes the males will groom the females to comfort them and get them relaxed this will also help the females become fertile.

After or once the offspring are born many of the young will stay with the parents up to 8 years old till they are ready to seek out their own mate, With Chimpanzee's the young will feed on their mother's milk up to the age of 5 years old. Depending on species of primates the weight of the young may be from 22lbs or up to 112lbs again depending on the species. And like most parents primates (human or non) are very protective of their young, Some will kill to defend them. Sometimes Killing even takes place when finding the mate.

This is some basic knowledge of the breeding process I will take you into more of the habits and behaviors that is very important to know as well as the Social behaviors in the known primate world.

VOCALIZATIONS , HABITS & BEHAVIORS

Although apes and primates are wild animals they have similar behaviors such as us humans in many ways as I will explain.

First of all we covered in the Breeding section that Primates remain or stay in groups some larger than others, Most of these groups are family based and although they have associated groups this does not stop them from wondering off alone to eat or mate. Some but not all primates are nocturnal and will go off at night and with various vocalizations they will sound off to notify others of their location; This is very common among many primates. Sometimes the vocalizations will indicate the call of a warning to let the group know of a predator that may be near. Chimpanzee's also chatter as well one of the main reasons behind a lot of their loud calls are a territorial thing . That's Something to remember or keep in mind .

USE OF TOOLS

This is a common trait among many primates but more commonly with chimpanzee's they use sticks to retrieve termites and ants from Dead trees or logs by dipping or sticking the stick in an opening and pulling it out with the insects covering the stick that was used to get the food. Leaves are another tool used for a few different uses, Such as to wipe their hands and yes even their Bottoms (Butts). That is Correct. They are very clean creatures and very smart. Leaves are also used as a sponge to absorb water and then squeezed to drink water from. Stones are used as a hammer to crack open nuts as well. All these uses of various tools are all signs of great Intelligence among the Known primates. They are not to be underestimated.

FOOD GATHERING

Chimpanzee's hunt in large groups and Cannibalism is all part of their eating and hunting habits . They hunt smaller monkey's as well as Baboons will hunt and take down antelope So for those that say its impossible that a Bigfoot will not eat a dear or that they are only Vegetarians guess again my friends , Primates are *Omnivorous* Creatures especially your Apes. A lot of primates including small monkey's eat crustations such as clams , muscles, and even crayfish , this is another reason why some primates stay near water. Other misc food sources for primates are Various insects , beetles, millipedes, crickets, and even birds. Tarsiers are small rodent like primates and are nocturnal and are *Carnivorous* and will not touch any Vegetation to eat. They are night hunters and will even eat small poisonous snakes.

MISC FACTS ABOUT PRIMATES

In this section I will make a recap of some of what I explained or discussed in earlier sections and add some other details that I have not covered. We see how highly Intelligent our known primates are and how they should not be underestimated by any means. Great strength in most primates is common especially with Gorilla's, Chimpanzee's, and the Baboon that can take down an Antelope , well Chimpanzee's have the strength to rip an arm off a grown man who even works out . One chimpanzee has the strength of at least 10 men or maybe more. I can quote from a true story That my father has witnessed from many years ago while attending a bar , a gentleman that came in with a Chimpanzee from a zoo on some occasions. The man was a zoo keeper but mainly in charge of looking after the Chimp , Well My father got to witness the following , the Chimp drinking beer and also the Chimp going against several different men in an arm wrestling matches and not one of them could even budge the arm of the Chimpanzee and at one point several men tried together all at once to take the chimpanzee down and even then could not do so. This was a true story and if this doesn't give you a clear illustration to show you the mighty strength of a primate then I can only tell you to get a clue.

On another note Chimpanzee's and other Apes have very little body fat and their bodies are made up of more muscle in Comparison to a Human. Because of this Apes do not have the ability to swim or float unlike us humans or some other smaller primates do. If a Chimpanzee was to fall in the water they would have the same affect as a rock fallen into the water, Going straight down.

To add a note about Scientist : they are still trying to figure out why some Monkey's have grown or "evolved" the way they did, I have found this most frustrating through my studies. WHY ? Because their theory of Evolution is a Joke and for those who follow it are as blind as they are. For all the matter just stop trying to figure out the natural take that was given to the natural order in which all became of what it was from the beginning and what is the same today.

Something Interesting to know that Experts in the Field of Primatology say it is hard to do Field Observations on a lot of the Primates especially Gorilla's , because they are shy animals and hide so well. If they are within site and move into the forest canopy they are pretty much gone. They are Experts at hiding . So we can most definitely agree when we compare our known primates with Sasquatch.

BEDDING & FORMATIONS

For most primates they build nests above the ground in trees consisting of other branches laid or sometimes woven together, Some Primates have adapted to build on the ground. Shelters vary , Some appear to be in a dome kind of like a pile of hey or grass but with Sticks , & tree limbs. If necessary other trees will be brought together in a tri-pod formation and the nest will be built on top this is known among a few of the great apes, Also for bedding they will also use Rock ledges and Cliffs. It is the stronger Primates who remain on the ground.

And as far as Formations found or made these may vary for the purpose . A lot of primates are very dominate and territorial and to show their Dominance at times they will break trees some of great size to show their strength to intimidate others.

(EXAMPLES FOUND DURING ECBRO FIELD RESEARCH)
with credits

ME

TRACY ARNOLD

ME & FRED

ME

ME

In the next but final section in regards to our known Primates pay special attention to what I discuss & share with you , It is Very important to both Known Primates and Bigfoot as you will read why .

ENDANGERED
(species)

Many of our primates are in great danger and for so many it is too late but If you do not know or are not aware of what is going on I am glad to tell you .
Primate Homes are being destroyed , What are their homes ? The Forests . Why ?
For temporary use of farming and growing crops. This is forcing Primates away from their natural habitat. And Primates are being hunted as well. A hunter will kill the protective parent of a young primate just to capture the young itself. Murder and Kidnapping !

WHAT ABOUT BIGFOOT – IS THIS SPECIES ENDANGERED ?

I believe very much so , Yes ! But there is something really wrong with this picture. The Government plays a key roll in this factor and I will try my best to explain and help you understand how and why this is True.

First of all our United States Government does not or will not acknowledge the Existence of the Species we know as Bigfoot or Sasquatch although other outside Governments do. When someone does come out openly with a claim with potential proof, These people are told or sometimes made to shut up or also told you did not see what you thought you saw. Interesting right ? Well its all about economic control and power.

To introduce an endangered species to our land that the Economy strives off of would put a stop or great hurt to the Economy itself. Back in the 1980's the spotted owl was discovered and immediately was declared an endangered species and what happened next was all the Logging came to a dead stop and till this day Logging is a big part of our economy for many uses . Now picture if an animal such as Bigfoot being so similar to a human appearance but yet a Primate become known and publicized can you imagine the Economic outrage that can take place and not to mention the many thousands of Individuals who would not be able to comprehend or be able to hold together the thought of such truth.
JUST THINK ABOUT IT......

A GREAT & GROWING TEAM

COME RESEARCH WITH US ; DO YOU WANT TO LEARN ABOUT THE OUTDOORS , OR EVEN KNOW HOW TO LOOK FOR BIGFOOT EVIDENCE COME JOIN US THROUGH OUT THE YEARS DURING OUR OUTTINGS & CAMPING TRIPS

WE ARE A NON – PROFIT ORGANIZATION AND OUR EVENTS ARE FREE.

Credits and other researchers

Dr. Jeff Meldrum

Loren Coleman

Fred Kanney

Tracy Arnold

Samuel Bell Jr

Cliff Stanley

Ian Redmond

John Bindernagel

Thank you to all these Gentlemen for their Research and Educational work for opening our minds into knowing the truth and guiding us all through dedication In the Bigfoot Community

All these Researchers Can be contacted Via email , Facebook or by phone see me for further details

REFERANCE SECTION FOR TRACK COMPARISONS

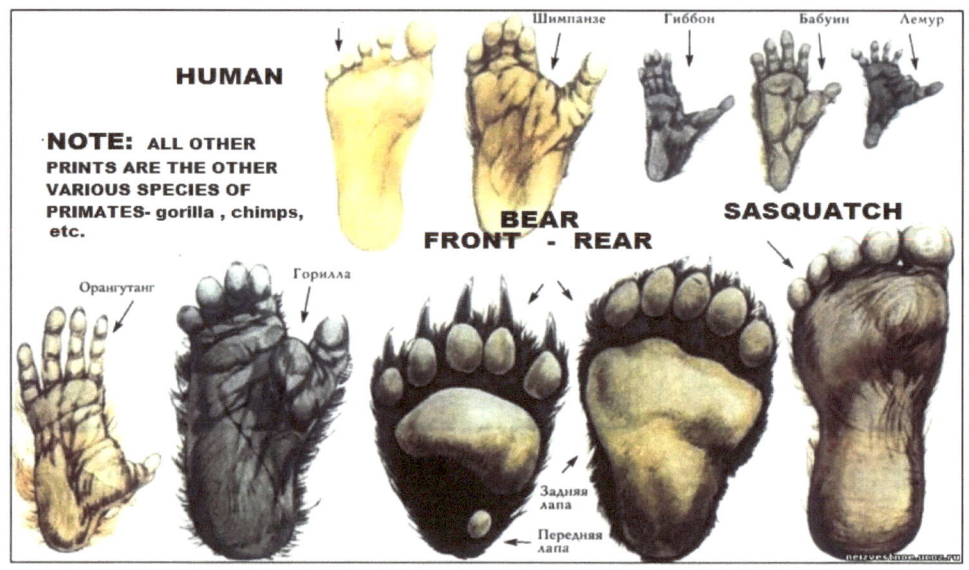

DERMAL RIDGE PATTERNS

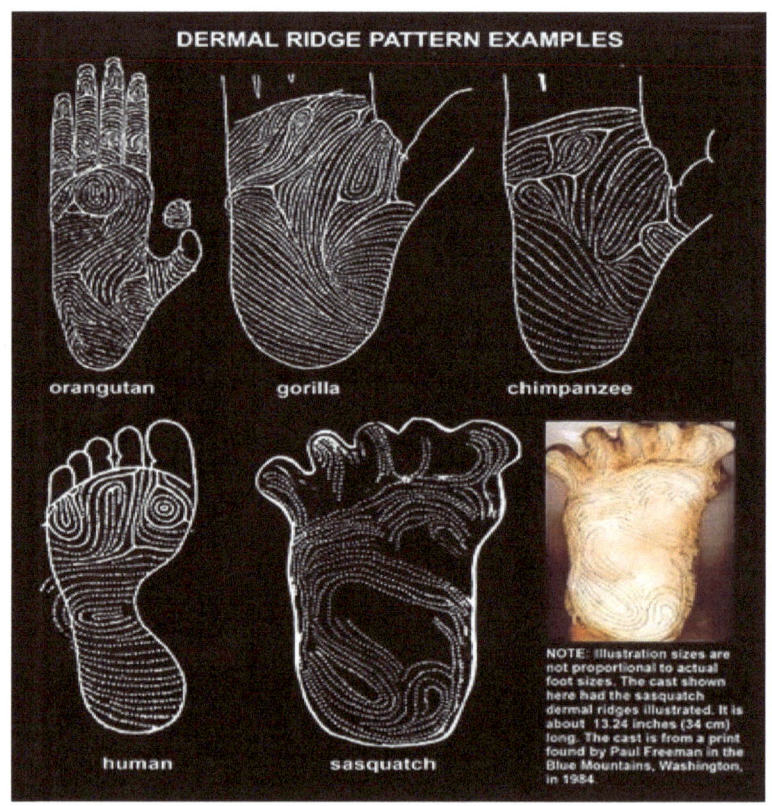

BASIC BIGFOOT

RESEARCH & GUIDE TO KNOWING THE

TRUTH

AUTHOR & RESEARCHER

Daniel Benoit

THE SOUL PURPOSE OF THIS RESEARCH BOOK

I put this book together for everyone both the Believer & Non , for the Bigfoot Enthusiasts , The skeptic and anyone Interested in the Subject itself and wanting a more clear understanding of what really is out there that so many ignore to realize. Everyone claims to know the truth if they exist or don't exist, well the Truth is they do but Not even I know or understand the complete truth , There is so much more to learn and know about these shy elusive smart creatures. We underestimate them to the point of not realizing that so much evidence is right in front of us but we need the right education to see it all. I shared some of my basic studies & research along with some simple illustrations to paint a picture in your mind of the truth. Everything in this book was shared for a purpose to compare and analyze with what is and was found in the field and so much more awaits us as we get out to discover. It is important to get out and understand the difference between our known wild life and what stands apart from what else is evident. I encourage you to start exploring nature and all of God's Beautiful creation. He has left so much mystery for us to discover. I am often brought to awe over the scenery he has set for us to love and ponder . Every day I am out there I find something new . Thank you for Reading and I hope my research and studies have shed some light on what you need to know.
God Bless,

Daniel J. Benoit